WARp oemS

Joe Donald Johnson

© Joe Donald Johnson 1974, 2018
Published by the author.
All rights reserved.
ISBN-13: 978-0-915564-12-5
ISBN-10: 0-915564-12-2

War Poems

Pages 7 through 45 hail directly from an earlier edition of this work (1974), written during the Vietnam conflict. The war produced a troubling rift in the American population. Pages 46 through the remainder are new and carry the dates of their creation. They are not focused on one particular conflict.

Contents

The War, January 17, 1970 7
We Have Brothers, We Have Sons 8
At Dawn They Were Born 9
A Salesman 10
The Orphan 11
They Say Men Die There 12
O to Be a Gutshot Lovely 13
Who Will Know when Gopo Dies 14
What Will Leon Baxter Do 15
Having Loved the Target, We Fire on Command 16
There Are Charlies on Both Sides 17
We Would Count the Dead 18
Powerless 19
Conscription 20
Man Walking 21
Commitment 22
Let Him Come Forward 23
All the Afternoon 24
So It Has Come to Be 25
Perhaps Our Lovers and Our Love 26
Perhaps in Love 27
If the Heart Cannot Hear 28
Call Your Love In 29
Field Hospital 30
How Will Time Leave All the Flowerets? 32
Deep in the Slumber of Blossoms 33
Before Raintime 34
Anthill—New Mexico 35
To Tell Her He Understands 36
The Students of Right 37
An Unheard Death in War 38
The AfterDeath 39
What Stands 40
We Newly Born 41
The General Statement 42
Smile Ol' Deathy Boy 43
The Gun Rises, the Gun Sets 44
The Way 45
Once upon a War in the Land of the Passing 46
Enemy Pines 47
Bluesburg, Graysburg 48
The Million Years War 49
Doss 50
The Stare 51
The Falling Memory 52
Grew a Battle 53
Spendthrift Bridge 54
Overthrow 55
Versailles 56
Crisis 57
Airstrike 58
The Child 59
Pregnant 60
Logistic 61
Luminary 62
Treaty 63

The War, January 17, 1970

Five planes a week
go down along the jungle border
down into the green disorder,
phantoms creep in the shade monsoon,
one is a white bone,
one a baboon,
the gunsights are willing
but the ghost eyes meek.

Beginning
is an ache in death.
How many lives a day
and every life an earth,
cease revolving on a battle axis
and lie so very still and placid
newborn to the moon?
Perhaps born happy after axes
after tactics
after acid.
Perhaps born joyous
into infinite time.
The hour was a casket.
The instant was a crime.

We Have Brothers, We Have Sons

And we are the children of good fathers.
Than those we love there are no others
Save for those beloved of others.
Who shall be the lonely ones?
Who shall be the bonely ones?
We have sons, we have brothers,
We have fathers, we have guns.

At Dawn They Were Born

At dawn they were born
and we stood them up in the dew
and we were ears for all their laughter.
We live longer, we live after.
Nothing wronger, nothing dafter.
Now is the one night long awaited
and hard fought for,
now is the night and they lie smiling
                  and they lie silent
                  and they lie reviled,
                            sublimely reviled:
laughter went crying
and the wind came wild.
We live longer, we live after.

A Salesman

A persuasive salesman L. Mort Enmity
rapped at the oaken door
and was asked in.
Now as though forevermore
we hate the enemy
we have never seen,
that same enemy
we have never been.

The Orphan

Every day in the afternoon
the four-year-old boy
with the eyes like rain
came to the barbed-wire city
to ask for food, food again
if anyone had pity.
If the soul is Beauty
and the soul is good
the soul is Horror
and the soul is pain.
One day the enemy,
the enemy ordained,
smiled and placed a patient hatred
in the boy's agent hand and said,
"Take this to the wire,
hold it tightly as you can,
and give it to the man."
The four-year-old boy
with the eyes like rain
came to the wire
and smiled and opened his hand.
The brain in him thought the fire.

They Say Men Die There

My neighbor disbelieves.
My neighbor says the suave suede men
in the elevated places
fabricate war
and the long toll of death
to carry our minds with carrion,
to win the approval
of our opinions with horror,
and that those long boxes they unload
from the yawning eagles of burden
are a cargo in vain—

whole islands of sand
to bury quiet and politic
under a hundred thousand
miniature white Calvaries.

O to Be a Gutshot Lovely

O to be a gutshot lovely
ravenhaired
small maiden dovely

weeping all the agony of Siam
whereon she lies

and O the I-want-to-be
that was once the I-am

so bravely burning, so brilliantly passionate
in her resigning eyes.

Who Will Know when Gopo Dies

Who will know when Gopo dies
that Gopo is dying
and Gopo is dead,
and who in hell was Gopo
with a name like Gopo
anyway?

What Will Leon Baxter Do

but what the mandate
and the scream
and survival
say to do?
What can Leon Baxter know to do
but to go forward,
forever forward,
though the fear fall dark,
and to have heard
no voices asking
who lives,
what thrives,
who dies?

Having Loved the Target, We Fire on Command

Because we once loved you
we now take aim.
Because we were your brothers
and your sons
we now conjure oblivions,
we now prepare our past
and fire.

There Are Charlies on Both Sides

One Charlie hides
and one Charlie ponders and decides
where to seek him out
beyond a shadow of a doubt,
this other Charlie who bears his name,
this other Charlie who shall bear his shame,
this other Charlie who shall lose the game.
But when this other Charlie dies,
triumphant Charlie need not write that name
(his own) over this other Charlie's grave:
Death is a god, a god has no grave.
And listen if you will into the wind that plies
open seas and summits of cold stone and whole skies
of stars: In Death is only Truth—no Charlie lies.

We Would Count the Dead

the many and very dead
if we could count.
And we would count
the tired and the unloved
the lost and the anguished
and the morally illegal
if these issues could count.
And we would count
one further flying eagle dawn
bleeding its ancient absent wing—
falling with the pauper,
falling with the king.

Powerless

We have seen with unresolved eyes
the fern grow final
in rocky mountain snow.
We and our blessed cause
were powerless after the claws.
Our cause was impotent with laws.
And we and our cause
were powerless with what Hatred knows,
powerless when the dustcloud rose,
powerless when the dust of peace
settled ashen on the frozen stares,
theirs
and their heirs'
and ours
and ours.

Conscription

Her dark hair poured the rain
the night he came to her,
though the sun would break the pools.
He lay at her side
like a toppled idol.
It was a world where geniuses and fools
were skulls for one harness
and mouths for one bridle.
He told her they had called to him,
from a dark place beyond murder
had called his name,
had answered the questions
of all his dissonant despairs of doubt
with his name again.

Man Walking

I see a man walking
in tearjerker smoke
bearing a torn banner
no one can read.
I see a man talking
no one can hear
all are asleep.
I see a man falling
in a mind-black cloud
clinging to the banner
weeps the war we bleed.

Commitment

My brother knows
it is I who am his enemy
and until duty
withdraws toward a flag
he knows he will murder me.
Yet he is aware of our brotherhood.
Forgive me for what I do to him
I do it for our brother good.
Forgive me the smile
barren of guile
and devoid of hatred,
he must behold before he kills.

Let Him Come Forward

Let him come forward,
him who is ordered
by the tongues of guns
to fuse the tons
of burst again,
to forge the horror
of piteous flesh
born poor, soon poorer,
soon poorer, soon poorer;
let us see him peer
into the mirror,
feel him fear
our tomorrow
and his fire.

All the Afternoon

All the long afternoon the live land's
rhythm danced the life's dance,
upheld the beat of the demonstration,
the drum of a new nomadic tribe
throbbing a novel kind of war-dream
to make an old hour new
and an old anguish end itself

but the old hour distrusting the motive.
Late in the long afternoon
the siren read
>   *How many are dead?*
>   *And are the dead*
>   *returning soon,*
>   *who said?*

All that endless afternoon
the migrant tribe played life and death
with an original pulse it thought it had heard:

>   *Peace! ... Now!*
>   *Peace! ... Now!*

Until the bloodstone swung away
(How many are dead?)
into the universal night
from its pocket of life and light
and secure warmth,
and stood again the whispering
watch of warriors
ignorant again beneath and over
and within and beyond
what is not known—
and a certain sentry comfort
the sudden whisperless moon.

So It Has Come to Be

So it has come to be. So it lives.
It came to be
out of a night unheard of
and unseen of
and it cried out passionately,
breathlessly,
           "I am, am I!"
So they called it "he"
but what could it be?
And they called Time time
but what could Time be?
Bone are the arms he ran to
and dust are the breasts he tongued.

Indeed it lives.
Impaled on the morphine
it screams insane to
no mind's ear, "I was, was I?"

So.
So what is a blinded eye?
So what is it to have been,
                      were you?
So what is it to become
                not you?

So its day is night
a night of mist.
So its unconsciousness cannot find Time.
And its secret heart
writhing away—
where can a heart wane to?

So it has come to be. So it lives.
So it will die a moment, and it lives.

Perhaps Our Lovers and Our Love

will die together
of one heart's pain
in the world's two weathers—
our lovers in the rain
far away,
and our love
(after sorrow)
some hopeless way
in the sun,
here, today—
or tomorrow,
say.

Perhaps in Love

Perhaps in love
there is pity.
Perhaps if one's belovèd dies
there is grief.
Not even love
can make a treaty.
Not even love's eyes
can change belief.

If the Heart Cannot Hear

Nothing is clear
but that the dead are dead
and the living are dying.
Nothing is dear
if the lovers there
and what they love here
die in the distance
between the abscess of absence
and the compress of fear.
If the heart cannot hear,
listens
which ear?

Call Your Love In

Call your love in and beware.
Worse than dying only once
is the loving done.
Worse than living only once
is the dying and the gone
disunison
of something loved:
that leaves the lover,
hand half in the glove,
not a finger anywhere.

Field Hospital

Here is a skeleton of boards
laid over with canvas
waterproofed with words.
It is called The End of the World.
Here is the policy: If it dangles
cut it off.
Here is the sanctuary
cadaverous and blessed.

They enter screaming from the war outside
                               the world outside.
There is pain to scream about.

They enter dying from the war outside.
There is damage
       pain
       and retreat
       to die about.

They enter dismemberment
from the blade without.
There is completion,
there is entirety
to be quartered from.

They enter dead
from the life behind.
There is birth to be dead from.

They enter consumed
with fear and with hatred
from the fire and the courage out of tent.
Hatred drove the man into the flame.
Fear brought the courage.
Fear and hatred are a storm
to find shelter from.

They enter moaning
from the great moan without.
There is the vast remigration of the wind
to bend into a moan with.

They enter remembering
from the hand of oblivion
throttling dominion without.
There is the sun
up yet, there is time
left in the breast
to remember the nurse.

The policy: If time dangles
cut it off.
        Sweep it out.
Call the little godlet who rates one stripe
to wash the place clean
of life's past power
devout enough to devour itself.

And they enter devoured.
A man remembered
among his people
for a single
ember of wisdom
gave the word:
There is rebirth to be dead toward.

How Will Time Leave All the Flowerets?

And how will Time leave all the buds?
The leaders have sworn all the flowers shall die,
flowers shall become as our sons and our brothers,
over whose perished pride
we drape our symbolic sorrow
and the weeping of our mothers.

How will Time leave all these little flowers
just born
must born?
(How large and how powerful
can a flower become after sun by the hourful
                           water by the showerful
                           air by the airful
and the fraught frontiers
          of years?
You cannot be too careful.)

All those flowerets, punk little flowers,
the leaders have sworn,
are going to buy it.
Not a leader will deny it.

And not a petal will defy it.

Deep in the Slumber of Blossoms

Deep in the slumber of blown blossoms past
Is a breathless perfect darkness vast;
Yet deep in the sleep of pistils past
An awesome burgeon dream is massed.
Should we sleep powerless could we sleep fast?

Before Raintime

Soon shall be raintime,
slowly comes raintime
an eon creeping.
How shall the eon rain,
what kind of eon rain,
and how much eon wind?
I peer into the distance
but I cannot discern,
I am sleeping.
Surely, I contend,
the children wars will end.
The tempest to come
shall rain and yet
with a touchless hand
burn fire, melt steel.

Peace then
to the dauntless will.
Peace to the gone pains.
Peace to the haunted slain.
Let what remains
be more in keeping
with the cause it rains—
a walless cause
a whispering cause
a warm cause weeping.

Anthill—New Mexico

and anthill— Vietnam.
They are flagrantly
common to two lands
which are one:
the everness of ants,
the ephemeral destiny
of the ant.

To Tell Her He Understands

he wakes to walk
along the East
River in mist
in hope of encountering
again that lady
he met in the mist of a year ago
who strolled in black silk
like a mere idea
carrying two candles
unlit unlit
one in each hand
and held them up before him
smiling her question:

"What sort of Power,
do you think,
excepting a match,
might fire these candles
in my hands—

"your smile,
do you think?
the end of the war?"

The Students of Right

In the quiet shade night
the students of right
are students of the fight
in which no might
can perpetuate
and from which all flight
is late.
Right is a blade bright.

An Unheard Death in War

He had been given birth for all tomorrows.
He had been given love, love had been given
To Life to make the present actual
With beings. In every creature and in stone
Slept the kinship. He had been given love
To rap the stone, and kiss the brow, and wake
The union into blossoming. For all
The ages gone had borne alliances—
Then burned the kiss, and severed off the stem,
Flooded the flower and frozen fast the root.
Love breathed a moment, winter sealed the vein.
But this new life was given birth to wake,
Not to sleep, to breathe for the stone but not
Become the stone. He had been given birth
For all the futures out of all the pasts
That hated so entirely that they ended.
The hatred in the stone became his present.
They gave him up to enemies and time,
They told his ear to kill the sound of Earth,
They told his eyes to blind the firmament,
They told his mouth to sing the gravensong
And speak the apt narrations of the guns.
No one could tell him that Unlife was None.
But fire could tell him that the stone was won.
And wind could tell him that the stone was long.

The AfterDeath

He had died
no man's death
but his own.
Laughless was the afterdeath.
Markless was the dark.
The only goldenwinged
cherub he chanced upon
told him he might lie by water
if he had loved more
than he had hated
when he lived;
and did not ask whom,
and did not ask how.

What Stands

What is it stands
between a man's
loves and a man's
lands,
between his shrewdness
and his glands,
between his rudeness
and his dance;
what is it stands
between a man's
condition
and his chance,
between his strangeness
and his change,
between cognition
and suspicion;
what can it be that stands
between a man's
mission
and his hands,
between petition
and demand,
between derangement
and exchange;
between his vision
and his glance
what is it stands?

We Newly Born

We, newly born,
are about to ask
where our eyes should be.
Do eyes have a task.
Does an eye have an enemy.
Does an eye have a past.
If an eye has a past
and if out of bygone urges
the crosshairs converge on life
just above the beating messenger,
what then of anger, most unblessèd
blinder of eyes?

We, lately warned,
are about to ask
what our eyes should see.
They are fixed fast
on our intention of persuasion,
resolved to apprehend without compassion
from the far promise of freedom
into the omnipotence of our inclination
the unbroken minds of our enemies.
We have appointed them our enemies.
We are about to ask
Can an eye grasp.

If truly born
we are about to ask
Can an eye cry
and should it and why.
Can eyes grow wise.
And if you kill an eye
          one eye
          nonborn
must the night
          not mourn;
and must the dawns die,
          no sky?

The General Statement

The General of Forces,
to disperse the perverse
curse the diverse
and reverse the universe,
has issued a statement,
he is quoted and syndicated:
"In the last election
too many weirdbeards voted.
We need to regiment
and recement
our forces.
Long live the legitimate.
Force will control the courts
and divorces."
Force will enroll the remorses.

The General of Forces
endorses purges,
blesses nurses
with scourges,
oppresses horses
and plays the hearses;
and has issued a statement.
What has he ever known
but hatement.
Who will lie down
at stiff "charade rest"
and play the dog's bone?
The Generous with Corpses
has issued a statement:
"People need to open their eyes.
What no one seems to realize
is this is the fourth and final quarter.
Call in the armor, bring up a mortar."
What someone dares to realize
is Lovely are the eyes
and Now becomes tomorrow.
Stave away the sorrow.

Smile Ol' Deathy Boy

Smile ol' Deathy boy ol' sot it's won
the dreaded round is shot
the kiddies are all patriot
paralyzed and begotdone

Smile ol' Death ol' soak ol' boy
weary is Life of eversplashing joy
weary is Life and irresolute
myopic and knockkneed and flat of foot
easy prey and feeble prize
and you are strongerful and wise
protocalled and authorized

Smile O Expunger of guys
smile for all the liddy eyes
of kiddies patriot
and tots for rot

What is vision but an eyeball trot
and what's the eyeball got
but what's down under the forgetmenot
cold
old
root
groaning for a truth of fruit,
untired of yearning
to push up thrust out
into good air what is yours ol' clot
and will come returning

The Gun Rises, the Gun Sets

Here is a timeless drum of tribes
Who wandered sunups long ago;
Telling all it can ever know
The drum is beating embryo.

With all the floodings of our sacred rivers,
With all the rushing of the blood that lives,
One with their rhythm, ere it ebbs
Our common pulse shall flow.

Here is a timeless drum of lives
Who wandered sunsets long ago;
Telling all it can ever know
The drum is beating overthrow.

The Way

There is one way:
You will fall into the pit
And die of it.
The day you quit
Is indefinite,
A day without time.
This is part of the way:
You will fall into the pit
And only die a bit.
You are infinite
And you sublime.
To go and leave all your love behind
You have only a summer
And an autumntime.
Winter is a glimmer,
Go emptied, be declined.

Once upon a War in the Land of the Passing

Life could have been
what it was in a while and a when.
But Death came then,
we know it yet,
came riding oxen,
riding horses,
riding elephants
in huge forces,
riding camelunds, oofinghoofs, helpfulants.
There were no talks in
the dust.
No safe walks in
arroyos.
There was neurotoxin
on arrows.
There were bleeding cottons
under armaments.
There were unspoken adoptions
in the hidden lands of the fledaways.
And there were weeping inscriptions
on standing stones
in the trodden gones,
in the optionless
silences of the dead away.

— January 27, 2018

Enemy Pines

There was a battle in a forest among living trees,
pines of many years, oaks of no fears, only constancies.
The battle was a killing of the living,
of hopes and dreams, and the men dropped lifeless,
abrupted screams, soundless requiems,
lad-shadows hidden, all giving given.
For the pines were firing upon both armies,
men peered for the enemy,
but pines, oaks, elms overwhelmed.
Yet men died, then men died,
then, when men died, men died.
And now their dreams, given once
to loves and truths,
now those dreams, red lies, lay,
and smoke drifted like the last of day
among their riven ruths.

— January 11, 2018

Bluesburg, Graysburg

And the scarlet of warletting,
creeks and bridges and fields of wheat,
churches, roads, burgs,
rises of rock
and a river of stone.
Bleat of creature,
nature in seizure.
And among the brigades
bayonet blades,
trades of volley,
memories of Molly
kissing in goodbye.
Now hue and now die.
One dies alone,
floating away silent
in the roar of corps,
in the crying among the violent,
toward asylum in the riot.

— January 28, 2018

The Million Years War

No one knew of it.
Dying came and went
and returned.
Birth yearned.
Fire burned.
And killing went spilling.
Ill did fulfilling fall.
Grieving did living heave.
To attack, the warriors
in their quiet crawled.
Victorious, defeated were they
for ours, for yours.
The hunters mauled.
Old grew few, old
grew none.
Then *pithecus* walked,
beholding the far horizon.
A million years of war,
no one knew of it.
It was merely life
scratching at life
to be life
and somehow,
by thumb's how,
do of it.

— *January 24, 2018*

Doss

Came Doss up the escarpment in 1945,
no weapon,
but a belief in a life unthreatened,
then hell welled up,
then the dying deepened,
and the wounds were bleeding,
and wounded need was needing, needing.
How to step in,
Doss, with hell deboning
and heaven unheard beckoning,
and the deafened ear unhearing?
A new aggression, Doss,
a belief in life unthreatened
came one Doss,
no weapon in Armageddon.

— January 11, 2018

The Stare

They called it the thousand-yard stare.
His photograph was snapped.
Yet there was no one there.
Battle Fatigue, a blitzkrieg waddle,
was a seated unreal ogle
of the unseeable.
The Stare has a different name now.
Post-Traumatic Stress Disorder.
After horror, no familiars, no ardor.
He stared away in a sweating frost
at nothing around him,
at some gun thing,
unremembering of routine.
He stared away into a distant horizon.
That horizon could not be envisioned.
The camera snapped.
Stone in his lone begone, enrapt
in his quietness strafed,
what he saw out there
was what he knew in here, him-within,
that what he had known
upon a once
was a bygone lost,
though before the troubling of the guns
it had been.

— February 5, 2018

The Falling Memory

Sighting down the M1,
firing all around me,
300,
400,
500 yards.
Downrange the metal man
rises from the trench,
uprange the nestled human Me,
unaddled,
finds level, finds sight, fires,
the metal man drops.
Firing all around me,
but no war,
only the before.
Only my M1 shoulder,
and off our shores
and far, far from the firing mound of me,
people getting older.

— January 14, 2018 ... a memory of 1960

Grew a Battle

Behind a hill above a place,
unknown to the place, grew a battle,
a shuffle-shoed quietness,
a lightness of weighted intent,
stealth swelling,
death gathering,
a certainty of slaughter,
a hurt-to-be reslaughter,
tomorrow's horror,
breath lathering,
rhetoric by projectile,
dying instant,
a killing of fathering,
to unlife an exile
of mothers distant.

— January 14, 2018

Spendthrift Bridge

They clashed in a sparking darkness
on a bridge,
tactics and courage
and surge
and cartridge,
and falling unalive.
Into sprawl without cry.
Their disputed ledge
suspended
over bleeding water.
More blood was spilled, spent with no thrift,
than either side comprehended.
The river below
the blood without sorrow
washed it with onward, with flow,
with some unshored forward,
with what a river knows
of tomorrow.

— February 5, 2018

Overthrow

Desperate, urgent
come the suppressed and insurgent,
and the killfire rattles
in narrow streets
in little battles,
they intend to supplant hatred
with hope, to avenge the lately dead.
The despot, leaning out at his window,
hears a breath afar
like screaming, like roar,
down narrow streets
toward a larger street,
a cityway death row
pitiless to be, O
a coming life-let,
drumming reprisal
and drumming yet,
hero and sparrow,
humming the war.

— *January 15, 2018*

Versailles

There was an entreaty of Versailles.
The question was Who heard?
And who heard the boots on cobblestone
on march in the future,
coming angry and endangering
and angling deathward
and measured and footsure?
If the ear refuses
then the future is soundless,
bringing its horrors countless
to confuse and surround us,
lit fuses, pursuers, newsless
slow gazettes, and off in the razed traces
graves unfound and dust.

— January 16, 2018

Crisis

What could be happening,
and can we understand?
It began in a day,
the bombs struck in a week,
and caustic ruin
brought a toxic dew in,
and people died.
They had lived with a certain happiness,
now their livingplaces are blackening,
and stunned to maddening they are,
but saddening beyond anger.
Flattening are their homes.
Damaged, their humanity.
Gunned to unhappening they are.
As ghosts they tread the way of war.
What can be happening,
and can we understand,
unmanned, unwomaned, unchilded
in a disbelief like damned,
like deminded,
like sand?

— January 23, 2018

Airstrike

Out of high mist, out of a wind
for jets, out of cloud,
out of death-intent
it comes.
Below, the enemy
is not known.
There, on earth,
friends are not known.
But the century
is of wing and of fire,
this is known.
Below, what entity,
enemy or friend in thee?
Nor governance nor embassy
speaks now.
What is known below,
under deathwind, under cloud,
an unlearning burn,
an unbecoming timelessly,
a devolving worldgone,
a horrid loud.

— *January 18, 2018*

The Child

Small steps.
Not far out, a dustwhirl.
Small steps,
boychild,
small steps,
girl.
The war away and near decrees
sentry duty, cleaning of weaponries,
cartridges many,
infinite distrust
of what the eye sees,
the distance, the wind and the dust.
The war near and away
war-ignores in the taut, bled and morbid today
the futures which ought,
the tomorrows of orchid and shore
and envisioning's blue rays,
small steps,
boychild,
small steps,
girl.

— *January 19, 2018*

Pregnant

The war-lightnings
are everywhere around,
florid brightenings,
torrid fightings,
lurid dyings.
There are ravines of screams
near and seeming,
out of scenes unseen
and unbelievable.
Under the rubble,
in her betroubled cavelet,
wrapped in waves of regret,
she is pregnant.
Her terror is for her fetus,
a terror of the outbled ceasings
in this infrared unquietness,
a terror for the child of childbirth,
its newbornness,
infancy,
toddling,
childness,
for the someday teen,
and by some mythic miracle,
may it be, pray it be,
the unenculted
adult.

— January 20, 2018

Logistic

Maneuver via this logistic:
Avoid the enemy.
Wait.
Believe hate
to be a length of fate
and the end of me.
Think your avoidance-logistic
mystic,
unlinguistic,
statisticless,
nonanalytic,
far-far from fascistic.
Far-far from ballistic.
Think it a dream futuristic.
Maneuver via this kissed logistic.
Avoid the enemy.
Wait.
Believe hate
to be a length of fate
and the end of thee.
Null and void is an avoided enemy.

— *January 22, 2018*

Luminary

With murder in their hearts
the gunners are seeking a luminary.
He envisions an end to the horror
endless in the winds, the horrors
aswirl toward dying in the darkness.
He dreams of a certain unwarring tomorrow.
He is therefore an enemy
of the gunners,
he somewhere blundering away
among the runners.
There is a light to him.
The people hide it in the night.
There is a kind of wonder
to him, a peace, a delving,
a hint at a helm,
an overwhelming
of the thunder.

— January 24, 2018

Treaty

In the chamber of relentings
the spokespersons
are eye to eye
that the war not worsen.
Though balm refuses,
there is a calm now,
infusing elocution.
Beyond, in the bombedness
of provinces,
the lamentings
will arrive as doves
in leafless birches,
as loves
in broken churches,
as grief overarching
demolished arches.
In the chamber of relentings
the paper takes pause
on a capable table.
There was cause
and anger,
hatred enwilding,
the dying and the dying away,
a world dechilding.
The peoples about,
surviving in the sway
of unthriving grief,
make gestures,
they are sequestered now,
and the long barrens of horizon,
so enlivened once
with dance and denizen,
are nonenvirons,
razed, without days, unrisen.

— January 21, 2018

www.ingramcontent.com/pod-product-compliance
Lightning Source LLC
Chambersburg PA
CBHW060722030426
42337CB00017B/2968